FRIENDS
OF ACPL

Americans All biographies are inspiring life stories about people of all races, creeds, and nationalities who have uniquely contributed to the American way of life. Highlights from each person's story develop his contributions in his special field — whether they be in the arts, industry, human rights, education, science and medicine, or sports.

Specific abilities, character, and accomplishments are emphasized. Often despite great odds, these famous people have attained success in their fields through the good use of ability, determination, and hard work. These fast-moving stories of real people will show the way to better understanding of the ingredients necessary for personal success.

Martin Luther King, Jr.

MAN OF PEACE

by Lillie Patterson

illustrated by Victor Mays

GARRARD PUBLISHING COMPANY
CHAMPAIGN, ILLINOIS

Dedicated to the gracious citizens of Atlanta,
to the members of Ebenezer Baptist Church,
and most especially
to the remarkable King family

Contents

1. Words and Walls

It was springtime in Atlanta, Georgia. Blossoms tinted the city with splashes of red and pink. A breeze blew across magnolia trees, dusting the streets and buildings with a scented breath.

On this spring day in 1933, Martin Luther King and two playmates romped together in his yard. "Catch it! Throw the ball higher! Bounce it harder!" Their voices blended together in childish delight.

Suddenly a voice called from across the street, "It's time to come home, boys."

"We're coming, Mother," Martin's two white playmates called back. "See you tomorrow, Martin." They dashed across the street to their father's grocery store.

Martin stood for a moment looking up and down Auburn Avenue. Negroes called this street "Sweet Auburn." It ran directly into downtown Atlanta. Some of the largest Negro-owned businesses in America were located there.

At 501 Auburn was Martin's sprawling two-story home. He stood in front of it, tingling to the exciting sights and sounds of the street. Lifting his face, he tossed his ball toward the blue sky. Sunlight slanted downward, kissing his almond-colored skin with warmth. Martin was happy. And whenever he was happy, he felt like singing. His voice sang out with the joy of being a four-year-old on a lovely spring day.

"Martin Luther King, Jr.!" His father called his full name from the front porch.

"You're going to make a fine preacher one day with that voice."

Martin ran to his father, who scooped the boy up and sat him on his knees. The Reverend Martin Luther King, Sr., seemed to his son as strong and sheltering as the giant oak tree in the yard next door. He was stout and solid, with an air of strength and firmness. Father and son sat together in a rocking chair, singing to the warm sun, to springtime in Atlanta, and to Auburn Avenue.

Martin was already singing solos in churches. His father was the pastor of the Ebenezer Baptist Church on Auburn Avenue. Martin's mother played the organ and directed the church choir. So Martin grew up singing.

Martin grew up loving words as well as songs. Every Sunday morning his father's booming voice retold the exciting stories from the Bible. Martin listened intently to the music made by the poetic words and phrases. He watched while his father made listeners sad or gay, angry or peaceful, all by the way he used words.

"You just wait and see," Martin told his mother. "I'm going to get some big words one day."

The King children also grew up knowing love. A sister, Willie Christine, better known as Chris, was a year older than Martin. Alfred Daniel, called A.D., was a year younger. Martin was called M.L. Although they had the usual childhood squabbles, anger never lasted in the King home. "There's nothing more important than loving one another," their parents taught them.

The children had Grandmother Jennie to run to when things went wrong. Mrs.

8

Ten-year-old Martin and his family

Jennie Williams, Mrs. King's mother, shared the twelve-room house with the King family. Her husband had been pastor of Ebenezer Church for 37 years. He died when Martin was only two.

Grandmother Jennie and Martin adored each other. She was able to chase away his childhood hurts with a kiss or a cheery word.

There was one hurt, though, that he could not easily forget. The two sons of the white neighborhood grocer remained his playmates until all three boys went to school. The grocer's boys went to one school, Martin to another.

One day when Martin ran over to play, the boys' mother met him at the door. "The boys can't come out to play today," she told him.

"Well, can they play tomorrow?"

"Run along home now, Martin."

The boys did not come out to play the next day, nor the next. Finally, their mother tried to tell Martin why. "You see, you are colored and they are white."

Martin ran to his own mother for a better answer. "Why?"

It was then that Martin found out about the "wall." Alberta Williams King took her son on her lap. She wiped the

10

tears from his eyes that had an Oriental slant. Slowly, patiently, she told him the story of slavery in America. She told of the days when proud black men were captured in Africa, brought to America, and sold as slaves. These slaves were often sold from owner to owner and looked upon as property, not as persons. Millions of slaves were sold in the South to work the large farms in that region.

"Slaves had no rights of any kind," Martin's mother went on. She explained that even though American Negroes had been free for nearly 100 years, they had never gained full equality. For the most part, white and black people continued to live separate lives, especially in southern states.

"But you are as good as anyone," Alberta King told her small son. "Remember this."

Martin remembered. As he grew older, he knew that an invisible wall seemed to separate the two races. The older a person grew, the higher the wall seemed to rise. Over and over again Martin read the signs that reminded him of this wall. *For Whites Only. Colored Entrance.* The words *Colored* and *White* separated drinking fountains, rest rooms, doorways, playgrounds, schools—the wall stretched endlessly. He learned another name for this separating wall—*segregation.*

In spite of this wall, Martin's life was happy. The nearby vacant lot was a perfect place for playing both baseball and football. The boys set up a homemade basketball court in the Kings' backyard. When they were not playing ball, they skated, shot marbles, flew kites, rode bicycles, and invented dozens of games.

Martin also spent many quiet times alone, for his father had a firm rule: "There is a time for play, a time for work, and a time for quiet reading and thinking." Martin would spend hours sitting in the shade of the backyard oak reading books. No wall separated friend from friend in books, and as he read, Martin Luther King, Jr., began to learn big words. One day he would use them as a weapon against the invisible wall.

2. A Family of Crusaders

Martin squatted behind home plate, catching balls and strikes. A ball whizzed into his mitt. "Strike three! You're out, A.D."

"That's ball two!" A.D. shouted back. "That ball missed the strike zone by a mile, M.L."

Sixteen other boys on the opposing baseball teams took up the argument.

"Ball two!"

"No, strike three!"

The voices grew louder. "Do you want to take to the grass about it?" one boy yelled. This was their signal to settle an argument by wrestling or fighting.

14

Martin faced his friends. "Calm down, fellows." He began to tell them, "Here's the strike zone. Here is where the pitch landed . . ." He talked on and on.

Finally the boys forgot about fighting. "You win, M.L. Let's play ball."

M.L. was very clearly the group leader. "M.L. can talk you into doing anything," his friends would say. "He *talks* his way out of trouble."

M.L. grew up knowing that his father, also called M.L., was a leader, too. He never forgot the day that Reverend King took him to a downtown shoe store. A salesman hurried to meet them. "I'll be glad to serve you if you'll just move to seats in the back of the store."

"There is nothing wrong with these seats," Reverend King said calmly.

"Sorry," said the shoe clerk. "We serve colored in the back."

"We'll buy shoes sitting here, or we won't buy shoes at all." Reverend King grabbed M.L.'s hand and stormed from the store. "I don't care how long I have to live with this system, I'll never accept it," he told his son. "I'm going to fight it until the day I die."

M.L. understood why his father had so much courage and pride. His father's early life was like a daring adventure tale.

Reverend King grew up on a sharecropper's farm in Stockbridge, Georgia. His father and mother worked hard from dawn to dark, year after year. Yet they scarcely made enough money to feed their ten children.

At sixteen, Martin, Sr., set out to seek his fortune in Atlanta. He worked by day and studied by night. After finishing high school, he entered Morehouse College and began to preach.

Meanwhile he met and married Alberta Williams. Her father, the Reverend Adam Daniel Williams, had built Ebenezer from a penniless church to one of the finest in Atlanta. He hired Martin, Sr., as an assistant pastor.

Martin, Jr., grew up knowing that his Grandfather Williams had also been a leader. He had helped to develop Auburn Avenue. He was a founder of the Atlanta branch of the National Association for the Advancement of Colored People. The NAACP was formed to help Negroes fight for justice and equal rights.

Reverend Williams crusaded to get a new high school for Negro students. A local newspaper printed hateful articles about the crusade. Reverend Williams answered by organizing a boycott, urging Negroes not to buy the newspaper. The paper soon had to close down.

Reverend King's crusading also became well known. He led the fight to give Negro teachers the same pay as white teachers. He joined the crusade that won Negroes the right to vote in the Georgia primary elections.

As M.L. grew older, he discovered other crusaders. He finished the sixth grade in public school, then entered a private school opened at Atlanta University. There he watched white and black teachers working together as a team. Many of the white teachers came from rich Northern families. They came South because they wanted to help train Negro students.

M.L. met the famous crusaders of history through his wide reading. He met the men and women, black and white, who crusaded to end slavery in America. His favorite hero of all was Frederick Douglass.

The years crowded one upon the other for the growing boy. He began selling newspapers to earn spending money. As much as his parents loved him, they never spoiled him. Theirs was a religious home. Each day began and ended with prayers. At the evening meal each child recited a Bible verse. Sundays were spent at worship services. "Ebenezer is like a second home," Grandmother Jennie often said.

She made M.L. her favorite grandchild and let everyone know it. One Sunday when M.L. was twelve, Grandmother Jennie was asked to speak at a Woman's Day program at a church. That was the day M.L. sneaked away from home to watch a parade on Auburn Avenue. A friend found him there and gave him the shocking news. "Your grandmother had a heart attack. She's dead."

M.L. dashed home, stunned and grief-stricken. From that day on he was a far more serious boy.

He studied much harder. At Booker T. Washington High School, he took part in public-speaking contests. One year his speech teacher took some of the students to compete against other students in Valdosta, Georgia. Martin won second prize. In a joyful mood, Martin's group boarded the bus for home.

Soon the bus grew crowded. "Move back!" the driver ordered the Negroes nearest the front. M.L. and the other students refused to move, even though they knew the Southern law and custom. Negroes sat from the back, white passengers sat from the front. If the bus became crowded, Negroes seated nearest to the front were forced to rise and give up their seats to whites.

"Move back, or I'll call the police!" The driver stood up.

M.L. could see the anger and hurt on his teacher's face. Yet she feared for their safety. "Please move, students," she said. "I don't want you hurt."

For her sake they moved. M.L. stood all the way. As he looked out the back window of the bus, he made himself a promise. "I'll be like Daddy. I'll fight this wall until the day I die."

3. Heroes and Honors

Martin stepped briskly across the tree-lined campus of Morehouse College in Atlanta. On his head perched a maroon-colored cap, a symbol that he was a freshman student. He had skipped two grades, so he was entering college at fifteen.

"Hi, M.L.," another student called to him. "How does it feel to be a Morehouse man?"

"It's the greatest feeling in the world," M.L. called back.

Morehouse College had been founded by a Negro minister in 1889. Many college presidents, ministers, and famous leaders had been trained at Morehouse. Now Martin King, in 1944, began his training in the traditional "Morehouse spirit." Students were taught three things: *You are a Morehouse man. You are as good as anyone. You are expected to be a success.*

M.L. enjoyed college life. He slept at home but spent most days on the campus. He sang in the glee club, and he joined friends in lively sports and parties.

Girls liked him. "That Martin King is a smooth-talking, fine-dressing, fancy-dancing freshman," they said. Boys liked him too. They nicknamed him "Tweeds" because he was so fond of wearing tweed suits and jackets.

M.L. made English and sociology his main subjects. English gave him increased skill with words. Soon he was winning first prize in oratorical contests. Sociology, the study of man, helped him to understand people. He did not know then how much his skill with words and his knowledge of people would help him in future years.

He always worked during his college vacations. Instead of taking easy jobs offered him by his father's friends, he worked with ordinary laborers. "I want to see how they live and feel their feelings," Martin said. Some of the Negro laborers who worked hardest were the ones with the lowest pay, the shabbiest homes, and the poorest schools. "Why?" M.L. answered himself. "It's the wall." Slowly a dream began to take shape. "I must do something to help these people. The wall must come down."

He made a decision. He told his mother first. "I am going to be a minister, like Daddy."

Martin Luther King, Jr., preached his first sermon in Ebenezer Church when he was only seventeen. By the time he finished Morehouse College at nineteen, he was assistant pastor to his father. That fall, M.L. entered Crozer Theological Seminary in Chester, Pennsylvania. The school had only six Negro students, but M.L. made friends with all 100 students.

He found his studies at Crozer exciting. Theology, the study of religious beliefs, helped him to understand the religious teachers of history. Philosophy, the study of wisdom and thinking, helped him to learn from great thinkers.

The young minister studied seriously the teachings of Jesus. *Love your neighbors. Love your enemies. Blessed are the peacemakers.*

M.L. sent this picture to Crozer Seminary with his application.

He was inspired by the life of his namesake, Martin Luther. This religious leader headed the movement that brought changes in church practices during the sixteenth century. Martin, the American, thrilled to read how Martin, the German, refused to recant, or give up his teachings. "I cannot and I will not recant anything," the other Martin had said, "for to go against conscience is neither right nor safe. God help me. Amen."

The writings of an American philosopher also fired M.L.'s imagination. Henry David Thoreau lived in Massachusetts during the mid-1800's. He had a fine education but took no interest in making money. Instead he tried to learn how social wrongs could be made right. Thoreau built a hut by a pond and lived there alone, studying nature and writing.

"If a law is unjust, men should refuse

to cooperate," Thoreau wrote. This refusal to cooperate is known as civil disobedience, and Thoreau himself practiced what he preached. He refused to obey laws he believed unjust, and willingly went to jail for acting on his belief. One man, Thoreau taught, can start a movement to bring justice, equality, and peace to the world.

M.L. learned that Thoreau's writings had crossed the world to India and inspired Mohandas K. Gandhi. Gandhi, born into a rich merchant family in India, studied law in England. India was then a part of the British Empire and had tried for years to gain independence. Gandhi decided to use Thoreau's ideas to develop a new way of fighting for India's independence. Gandhi's method was based upon courage, love, and nonviolence.

Some people called Gandhi's method peaceful protest, or nonviolent resistance.

Gandhi called it "love-force." The manner in which a person behaves, Gandhi taught, is as important as what he achieves.

Gandhi freed himself from all fear, lived a simple life among the poor people of India, and taught them fearlessness. Thousands of Indians followed their gentle leader, calling him the *Mahatma,* meaning Great Soul.

Gandhi and his followers protested unjust conditions with mass marches, boycotts, strikes, and daily prayer meetings—but always in a spirit of love. They were beaten and jailed, but they never fought back with violence or weapons. "I want to touch your hearts," Gandhi told the British officials. "Only then will you change."

They did change. India gained independence from Britain in 1947. Sad to say, Gandhi was assassinated the next year while he was leading a prayer meeting.

The teachings of these great men helped Martin Luther King to form his own philosophy of life. It was a philosophy based upon courage and love.

Martin graduated from Crozer in 1951, leading his class with an A average. He won the award as the most outstanding student, along with a scholarship of $1,200 to continue his studies. First though, he returned to Atlanta. His father had promised to let him run Ebenezer all by himself during the summer.

4. Coretta

It was autumn in Atlanta. M.L. packed his books and clothes in the new green car his parents had given him for graduation. He headed the car toward Boston, Massachusetts.

At Boston University he began his studies toward the Doctor of Philosophy degree, the highest research degree in America. He also took courses at Harvard, the university that Thoreau had attended.

Another student arrived in Boston that fall. Coretta Scott came from Heiberger, Alabama. Her hard-working parents did not have much money, but they were determined that their three children would get good educations.

They sent Coretta to nearby Lincoln School, run by church missions since the 1860's, with white and black teachers. The gifted Negro music teacher, Miss Olive J. Williams, took a special interest in Coretta and helped her to develop her musical talents.

After high school, a scholarship helped Coretta to attend Antioch College in Ohio. When she graduated, another scholarship enabled her to enter the New England Conservatory of Music in Boston.

So the theology student from Atlanta, Georgia, and the music student from Alabama met in Boston. They studied each other seriously the day they met. Coretta saw a young man, five feet seven, with broad shoulders and powerful legs.

She liked his gentle manner and his friendly smile beneath the trim mustache.

M.L. could not take his eyes off the girl with honey-brown skin and dazzling smile. Her long, curly hair framed a pretty face with upward-tilting nose. As they talked during lunch, he was delighted to learn that she was a wide reader too. "You can *think* as well as sing," he teased. "You can talk about *ideas*."

Over the next weeks they learned more about each other. Coretta listened as M.L. talked of his big dream. "I want to help poor people so they can help themselves." It was hard for her to understand why he felt so strongly about poor people. He had never been poor himself.

Coretta talked about her early life. As a young girl, she had been a fighter, not a talker. It was hard for M.L. to believe that the poised young lady had once been

35

Coretta and Martin on their wedding day

a tomboy. "You have all the qualities I would like to find in a wife," he told her.

Coretta faced a big decision. She had worked and studied hard to become a concert singer, not a minister's wife. She had a dream too. She dreamed of singing in crowded halls with applause ringing in her ears.

Coretta decided to join the young minister and share his dream. On a June day in 1953 the two were married in the garden of Coretta's family home in Alabama. Reverend King, Sr., married them. Martin's brother, A.D., was best man. Coretta's old friends and neighbors came from all around to see the young minister she had chosen instead of a concert career. They liked what they saw.

The new husband and wife set up housekeeping in Boston and finished their studies. Now, to win his degree, M.L.

needed only to write the long research paper called a thesis.

It was time to look for a job. Would it be in a college or a church? North or South? Many good offers came. Dr. Mays invited M.L. to teach at Morehouse. Another interesting offer came from the Dexter Avenue Baptist Church in Montgomery, Alabama.

Coretta and Martin King both knew the problems they would face in the South. They also knew the promise awaiting them there. "Something wonderful is unfolding in the South," Martin said. "I want to be part of it."

They went South to Dexter Church and Montgomery.

5. "My People Are Tired"

The sound of singing filled the white frame house. Coretta King sat at the piano, her well-shaped fingers skimming over the black and white keys. Her clear soprano voice followed the fall breeze through the open doorway.

Martin King sat in his study. He enjoyed listening to his wife practice her music while he worked. The Kings were happily settled in their home in Montgomery. Martin spent part of each day working to finish his 343-page thesis.

Some members of the Dexter Avenue Baptist Church at first thought that their

Dr. King greeting churchgoers at Dexter

minister was too young. "He looks more like a college student than a preacher." They changed their opinion when they heard him preach.

The year 1955 was a happy time for Martin and Coretta King. Martin received his doctorate from Boston University. He was now *Dr.* King. Five months later their first baby was born. They named her Yolanda Denise but nicknamed her Yoki.

40

Dr. King was happy, but his dream was not forgotten. The wall of segregation in Montgomery was strong and rigid.

One of the biggest problems was the city bus line. It had the segregated seating pattern, with something extra. The first four front seats were "reserved" for whites. Negroes were *never* to use them. Anyone who protested was threatened, beaten, or jailed. Yet 70 per cent of the bus riders were Negroes.

Suddenly this all changed on Thursday, December 1, 1955. Mrs. Rosa Parks, a sweet-faced seamstress, boarded a downtown bus. She was tired from sewing all day in a department store. Mrs. Parks took a seat behind the "reserved" section.

The bus rolled along. More white passengers got on. The driver ordered Negroes sitting near the front of the bus to stand. Rosa Parks sat. "I am tired,"

she told herself. "I can take it no longer."
The driver called a policeman. Mrs. Parks
was arrested and taken to jail.

News of the arrest crackled over the
telephone wires like a forest brush fire.
"We are *all* tired," Negroes told one another. An idea formed and spread from
phone to phone. "Boycott the buses!"

The next four days brought an exciting
drama.

Friday. Civic leaders met in Dr. King's
church to plan a one-day bus boycott.

Saturday. Dr. King and his church
secretary worked all morning preparing
leaflets. An army of women and students
took these 7,000 leaflets to the Negro
families in Montgomery. *"Don't ride the
bus to work, to town, to school, or any
place Monday, December 5."* The leaflets
also invited everyone to a mass meeting
the following Monday night.

Sunday. Dr. King and most of the other Negro ministers preached the message from their pulpits.

Monday morning. Dr. King and Coretta were awake by 5:30. They watched a bus pause at the bus stop a few feet from their house. "Martin, oh Martin, look!" Coretta exclaimed. She pointed to the bus. "Darling, it's empty!" So was the next bus, and the next.

Dr. King jumped into his car and drove around the city. Most of the buses were empty. He saw Negroes walking, walking, walking. "A miracle has happened," he said.

Monday afternoon. Negro ministers and other civic leaders formed a group to direct the movement. One white minister, the Reverend Robert Graetz, joined them. The Reverend Ralph Abernathy, Dr. King's best friend, suggested a name for the

group: The Montgomery Improvement Association, or MIA. Dr. King was elected president.

Monday night. Dr. King gave the main speech at the mass meeting. The church was packed. More than three thousand people stood outside to listen.

"There comes a time when people get tired," Dr. King preached. *"Tired, I say. Tired!"* The young minister threw out a call for action but gave rules on how to act. "Love must be our regulating ideal."

Dr. King's voice swelled like a mighty organ, calling forth a chorus of courage and compassion. "If you will protest courageously, and yet with dignity and Christian love, when the history books are written in future generations, the historians will have to pause and say, 'There lived a great people—a black people—who injected new meaning and dignity into the veins of civilization.' This is our challenge and our overwhelming responsibility."

Listeners roared their approval. "Continue the boycott! Keep on walking!"

And they did. "That night was Montgomery's moment in history," Dr. King wrote. It was his moment in history too.

6. "Our Weapon Is Love"

"Walk straight! Walk the streets of Montgomery until the walls of segregation are battered by the forces of justice." Dr. King preached courage to Montgomery's 50,000 Negroes. The bus boycott became a walking, singing, praying crusade.

The boycotters walked through the cold of winter, the rains of spring, and the blistering heat of summer. Volunteers formed a car pool of more than 300 cars. Each Negro church bought a station wagon.

Dr. King patterned the crusade after Gandhi's nonviolent movement in India.

"I used the teachings of Jesus to give spirit to the movement," he said. "I used the methods learned from Gandhi and Thoreau." Like Gandhi he freed himself from fear, then taught fearlessness to his followers.

Dr. King realized that the Negro race had a long tradition of deep religious faith. He used the weekly mass church meetings as a time for teaching his special lessons. "Our weapon is love. Hate cannot drive out hate. Only love can do that."

He taught the meaning of nonviolent resistance. "It does not seek to defeat but to win understanding and friendship." The movement was not against persons, he stressed, but against an evil system. "You must be willing to suffer the penalty for your resistance. Above all, you must be willing to go on loving those who make you suffer."

Walking was a symbol of freedom.

City officials thought the boycott would fizzle out in a few days. "Get tough!" they ordered.

Policemen began threatening car-pool drivers and giving them traffic tickets. Some were even arrested. Dr. King himself was arrested one day and taken to a crowded jail cell. When the jailer saw a crowd of angry crusaders coming toward the jail, he quickly freed his prisoner.

Dr. King went home to Coretta and Yoki. At home the phone rang all day and well into the night. Many calls brought threats of death.

One night in January, while the boycott was still in full force, Dr. King spoke at a church meeting. Terrible news reached him there: "Your house has been bombed."

"Are my wife and baby all right?"

"We're checking on that now."

Dr. King rushed home. The bomb had damaged a part of the porch and shattered the windows. Inside, the Mayor of Montgomery and other officials were gathered, surveying the frightening scene. Dr. King breathed a sigh of relief when he saw that Coretta and Yoki were safe.

Outside, more than 1,000 angry, shouting Negroes circled the house. They refused to leave. An official turned to Dr. King. "Please send them home."

Dr. King faced the outraged crowd. He knew that they were in a mood to rip

the city apart. He raised his arm. "If you have weapons, take them home." His face showed sadness, not anger. "We must meet hate with love. Leave peacefully. If I am stopped, this movement will not stop, because God is with the movement."

The crowd grew silent with awe. They could now see their leader's teachings in action. His wife and baby could have been killed. Yet he stood there talking about love and forgiveness.

An old man broke the silence. "God bless you."

"Amen! Amen!" came from the crowd.

The next month city officials arrested about 100 boycotters. They included Dr. King and most of the Negro ministers in the city.

Dr. King was found guilty of disobeying an old anti-boycott law. He asked for a new trial. As he walked from the courthouse, newsmen met him. "Will you continue the boycott?"

"The protest goes on!" Dr. King vowed.

"Hail the King!" someone called from the crowd.

"King is *King!*" the crowd answered.

The protest leaders had been asking only for more equal treatment on buses. Now they decided to ask the federal courts to end all bus segregation in Montgomery.

These events proved turning points in the life of Martin Luther King. He became an international hero. Newspaper and

Even in troubled times, home with Coretta and Yoki was full of joy.

television reporters flocked to Montgomery. The world watched the day-by-day happenings in the city.

Gifts of money poured in from all over the United States and from foreign countries. Dr. King traveled about the country, telling the Montgomery story. Coretta gave concerts to raise money.

Finally, after 381 days, the boycott ended. The Supreme Court of the United States ruled that the bus segregation in Montgomery was unlawful.

The movement ended, as it began, with a mass rally. When Dr. King entered, the people stood, cheering and weeping.

The blond Reverend Graetz read from the Bible. "When I became a man I put away childish things." The weary crusaders knew that they had grown stronger over the past year. They were *equal!* No signs would ever tell them differently.

"Accept your victory with humility," Dr. King taught them. "Do not boast. Be loving."

Early one December morning, Dr. King boarded a bus. The white driver smiled. "I believe you are Reverend King, aren't you?"

"Yes, I am."

"We are glad to have you this morning," the driver said.

Dr. King thanked him and sat down in one of the front seats.

7. Stride Toward Freedom

By 1957 Martin Luther King, Jr., was one of the most sought-after speakers in America. He traveled thousands of miles and spoke more than 200 times each year.

One trip took him to Ghana, in Africa. Dr. King went as an official guest along with Vice-President Richard M. Nixon and other dignitaries. They attended ceremonies celebrating Ghana's birth as an independent nation. Dr. King came home with a stronger belief in his dream of full freedom for black Americans.

He gained added inspiration from the flood of medals, awards, and honorary degrees. Coretta later turned one wall of their home into a "Wall of Fame." Visitors could see the awards and read the words used to describe her husband—courageous–fighter–scholar–builder–gentleman.

Dr. King snatched time from his busy life to enjoy his growing family. Yoki, with her father's Oriental eyes, looked like a little doll. Another baby, Martin, III, called Marty, was born in October, 1957.

The crusading dreamer used his writings together with his speeches as weapons against injustices. His first book, *Stride Toward Freedom*, told the story of the Montgomery crusade. In September, 1958, Dr. King came to a department store in New York City to autograph copies. He laughed and joked with the crowds as he signed his name in their books.

Suddenly a dark-skinned woman pushed

through the crowd. Before anyone could stop her, she plunged a letter opener into Dr. King's chest.

"No! No!" Some people in the crowd began screaming and rushing about. A woman reached to pull the weapon out. Someone seized her hand in time. "You'll kill him! Wait for the doctor."

Dr. King was the calmest person of all. He sat still, not speaking, not moving. He had trained himself to stay calm in the face of violence. Now this training saved his life. A doctor explained later the dangerousness of the situation. "He was a sneeze away from death." The tip of the eight-inch weapon rested against the big heart vein. If Dr. King had coughed, sneezed, or twisted his body, he would have died at once.

Doctors took hours to open his chest and gently remove the letter opener. For some time no one knew whether Martin Luther King, Jr., would live or die.

After the long illness caused by the attack on him, Dr. King decided to travel to India, the land of Gandhi, for inspiration. How the Indians loved the King family! Coretta graciously sang for them. Dr. King traveled about India, giving speeches and talking with the people. "To other countries I may go as a tourist,"

A visit with India's Prime Minister Nehru

Gandhi's portrait hung in Dr. King's study.

he told them. "To India I come as a pilgrim." He made a solemn pilgrimage to the shrine of Mohandas Gandhi.

Back home, job offers of all kinds awaited Dr. King. He could have become wealthy overnight. He had other dreams, though. He felt certain that he could use love-force to change America into a land of full equality for all men.

Dr. King and some other ministers had already formed the Southern Christian Leadership Conference, often called by its initials, SCLC. This important group planned to spread the struggle for equality to all states. Dr. King was its president. He decided to return to Atlanta, preach part time at Ebenezer, and direct the SCLC freedom movements.

Sorrowfully he asked the members of Dexter Church to let him go. "I can't stop now," he told them. "History has thrust something upon me which I cannot turn away."

The members of Dexter learned that they, like Dr. King's family, had to share him with the world. Martin Luther King, Jr., had to "stride toward freedom."

8. "We Shall Overcome Some Day"

Dr. King's dream caught the imagination of young people. Students met at colleges and talked about his courage.

On February 1, 1960, four Negro college students sat at a lunch counter in Greensboro, North Carolina. They politely asked for service. They were firmly refused. Instead of leaving, the students opened their books and began to study.

The next day they returned with more students. This action began the sit-in crusade to end segregation in eating places. The idea spread from campus to campus with the swiftness of an atomic chain reaction. White students from all parts of the country came South to join black students in their crusade.

Dr. King became an adviser to the student leaders. He helped them to form their own group, the Student Nonviolent Coordinating Committee, called SNCC.

Sit-ins were held at lunchrooms in many department stores. Dr. King joined the students in a sit-in at Atlanta's biggest

department store. He was arrested and sentenced to hard labor in a prison camp.

Small Yoki heard the news and ran to her mother, weeping. "Someone said Daddy is in jail. Why?"

Coretta tried to explain "why," exactly as Dr. King's mother had done when he was young. "Your Daddy went to jail to help people. You know some people don't have nice homes to live in, good food to eat, or clothes to wear. Your Daddy is trying to help people get these things." Yoki dried her tears.

Dr. King's arrest had a dramatic effect upon the 1960 Presidential election. John F. Kennedy was running a close race with Richard M. Nixon. Mr. Kennedy telephoned Coretta. "I'll do all I can to help." His brother Robert helped too. Largely because of their efforts, Dr. King was released from jail.

Dr. King and John Kennedy became friends.

Negroes were touched by the concern of the two rich and famous brothers. Most of them voted for John Kennedy, who won by a small margin. So the course of history was changed because Martin Luther King took part in a sit-in.

The sit-ins led to freedom-rides. White and black "freedom riders" rode together through southern states, ignoring the *White* and *Colored* signs. They knew that many riders would be mobbed, and some killed. They willingly filled the jails, singing freedom songs.

"We Shall Overcome" became the rallying song of the freedom movement. The song is based upon an old gospel hymn, with new words and music. It was sung in jails, on marches, and always in times of danger or triumph.

All the civil rights groups worked together to help direct the new crusades. It was Dr. King, however, who became the symbol of the movement for equality. Whenever a crusading group faced discouragement, Dr. King rushed to cheer its members with a speech.

One night about 1,000 freedom riders met for a rally in an Alabama church. Dr. King gave the main speech. A howling mob of segregationists surrounded the church, threatening to kill everyone inside.

Robert F. Kennedy was then Attorney General of the United States. He stayed by the telephone all night in Washington, D.C., arranging protection for those at the rally. United States marshals, officers of the federal courts, were rushed to the church.

Inside the church, Dr. King was able to keep everyone calm with the magic of his oratory and the example of his firm faith. All joined hands together and sang.

We shall overcome, we shall overcome,
We shall overcome some day.
Oh, deep in my heart I do believe
We shall overcome some day.

They overcame. Federal marshals led Dr. King and his freedom riders safely from the church as a new day was dawning.

WE SHALL OVERCOME
New Words and Music Arrangement by Zilphia Horton,
Frank Hamilton, Guy Carawan & Pete Seeger
TRO © Copyright 1960 and 1963 LUDLOW MUSIC, INC.,
NEW YORK, NEW YORK. USED BY PERMISSION.
Royalties derived from the composition are being contributed to
the Martin Luther King Fund under the trusteeship of the writers.

9. "Letter from a Birmingham Jail"

The year 1963 marked 100 years since slavery had ended in America. Dr. King chose that year to lead some of his boldest protest movements.

Birmingham, Alabama, was known as the most segregated big city in America. Dr. King called for volunteers to help him dramatize the injustices there. Each volunteer had to attend workshops and learn nonviolent methods. Each signed a pledge: "REFRAIN from the violence of fist, tongue, or heart."

The drama unfolded at the beginning of the Easter season. Men and women dressed up in their Sunday clothes and marched through the streets in peaceful protest.

Birmingham's tough police commissioner met the marchers. "We'll fill up the jail!" he said.

The marchers did fill up the jail, singing as they went. Dr. King was arrested on Good Friday and placed in solitary confinement.

He spent Easter Sunday in jail, thinking and praying. He thought about a letter that white ministers in Birmingham had written, criticizing his crusade.

From the dark, cheerless jail cell, Dr. King answered them. "I am in Birmingham because injustice is here," he wrote. He explained, in a spirit of faith and brotherhood, why Negroes could no longer wait to gain equality. The 9,000-word "Letter from a Birmingham Jail" was

later printed. It became a modern classic. Many people thought of Thoreau's famous essay "Civil Disobedience" as they read it.

Dr. King came out of jail to face a fateful decision. The young children of Birmingham were eager to join the freedom crusade. Could he let children join, Dr. King wondered. For three nights he stayed awake worrying. At last he gave the word: "The children may join!"

On a sunny May day, an excited army of children streamed from a church and paraded downtown. "March, march, march for freedom!" they chanted.

Enraged policemen set upon them with billy clubs and snarling police dogs. Countless children were carried to jail. Twice as many took their places the next day. Grown-ups joined their youngsters.

"Turn on the fire hoses!" ordered the police commissioner.

Streams of water from high-pressure hoses ripped into the marchers. The pressure was strong enough to rip bark off trees. "Freedom!" youngsters cried out as the water battered them to the ground. No physical force was strong enough to defeat Dr. King's weapon of love-force.

The scenes in Birmingham, pictured in

newspapers and on television, filled the nation with horror. Hearts changed, even hearts in Birmingham. City officials agreed to give Negroes better jobs and to desegregate public places. Much of the success of the crusade was due to the courageous children who took part.

The Birmingham crusade inspired freedom movements in more than 1,000 towns and cities. Behind them all was Dr. King—speaking, writing, advising, and giving inspiration.

The dramatic events of 1963 climaxed with the biggest freedom demonstration ever staged in America. This March on Washington, planned by all civil rights groups, came in the late summer.

10. "I Have a Dream"

August 28, 1963, dawned clear and golden in the nation's capital. Dr. King woke up early as he always did. His plans for the March were all set. So were plans for his meeting later that day with the President of the United States.

President Kennedy shared Dr. King's dream of full equality for all Americans. In June he had asked Congress to pass a broad civil rights law. The March on Washington dramatized the need for all Americans to support the enactment of this law and work to break down segregation walls.

Marchers came in car pools, buses, trains, and airplanes. Some came on foot as "freedom walkers." An old man pedaled from Ohio on a bicycle. A young man skated from Chicago, Illinois. Crippled marchers hopped on crutches and rolled along in wheelchairs. The blind held the hands of those who could see. Children skipped along in the color and excitement of the day.

By noon the marchers wound like a multicolored ribbon toward the Lincoln Memorial. Millionaires marched beside sharecroppers, foreigners beside Americans, blacks beside whites. Shoulder to shoulder, hand in hand, they marched in friendliness and equality. At least one-fourth of the marchers were white. Dr. King described this strange and noble army: "It was a fighting army, but no one could mistake that its most powerful weapon was love."

The whole world watched. Television cameras recorded the day-long drama. Stars of the entertainment world performed for the crowd. Excitement mounted as the main program began. The speakers were impressive. The songs were soul-stirring. The excitement became electric when the main speaker was announced: the Reverend Dr. Martin Luther King, Jr.

He stood framed by the statue of Abraham Lincoln and flanked by the American flag. The years of crusading had stamped a look of gentle sadness upon his face.

For 100 years, he began, Negroes had carried in their hearts the hope of full equality in America. Now was the time to fulfill the promises of democracy.

Dr. King's voice was like a well-tuned instrument played by a master musician. "I still have a dream. It is a dream deeply rooted in the American dream."

"I have a dream . . ." Over and over the crusader chanted his dream for the Negro and for a better America. He held listeners breathless with rhythmic, rolling phrases. As he ended, his voice soared toward the white-domed Capitol. "Let freedom ring!" He voiced the hope that one day all men would live the meaning of the old slave song. "Free at last! Free at last! Thank God Almighty, we are free at last!"

The marchers were caught up in the wonder and beauty of the moment. Men and women, even news reporters, wept openly. Others miles away wept beside their television sets. Trees shook with the thundering applause given the gentle dreamer. The music of freedom floated over the reflecting pool.

Oh, deep in my heart I do believe
We shall overcome some day.

Dr. King had given his dream to the nation. It now became an all-American dream.

WE SHALL OVERCOME
New Words and Music Arrangement by Zilphia Horton, Frank Hamilton, Guy Carawan & Pete Seeger
TRO © Copyright 1960 and 1963 LUDLOW MUSIC, INC., NEW YORK, NEW YORK. USED BY PERMISSION.

11. "I've Been to the Mountain Top"

"Daddy's home! Daddy's home!" Dexter chanted as Dr. King came up the steps.

"Daddy, can we go swimming together?" asked Marty.

"I've learned a new song since I saw you," whispered Yoki. Baby Bunny held tightly to her father's finger.

The King household bounded with joy whenever "Daddy" came home. There were now four children. Dexter Scott, born in 1961, was named for the Alabama church where Dr. King gained fame. Bernice Albertine, nicknamed Bunny, was born only a few days before the 1963 Birmingham crusade.

The children adored their famous father. Away he was their hero; at home he was their playmate. The living room often became a play area where Dr. King romped on the floor with them. A picture of Gandhi on the wall looked down upon many a rollicking scene.

The Kings packed as much fun as they could into the days they had together. Sometimes they gathered around Coretta at the piano for song sessions. Sometimes Dr. King played the piano. His favorite hobbies were music and swimming.

The children were taught to share him. "Daddy's away helping others," Coretta would explain. "When he's finished, he'll be back." Dr. King gave them the experience of walking in "freedom marches." When other children went without new toys or clothes because of boycotts, the King children did so too.

Martin Luther King plays
with Yoki (left). Below,
four lively children—Yoki,
Bunny, Dexter, and Marty
sing with their mother.

Dr. King preaching at Ebenezer Church

The members of Ebenezer Church un-
selfishly shared Dr. King also. They knew
that their beloved M.L. would preach for
them as often as he could. They prayed
when he faced danger and rejoiced when
he won honors.

They rejoiced when *Time* magazine
voted Dr. King "Man of the Year" for
1963. They again rejoiced in 1964. Dr.
King watched as President Lyndon B.

Johnson, who took office when John F. Kennedy was assassinated, signed the new Civil Rights Act. Mr. Johnson shook Dr. King's hand and presented him with one of the pens used in the signing.

Greater rejoicing came when Dr. King won the 1964 Nobel Peace Prize. At 35 he was the youngest person ever to receive this award. His family and many of his friends flew to Norway with him.

The chairman of the Nobel Peace Prize Committee presented the award. He called Dr. King "the first person in the Western world to have shown us that a struggle can be waged without violence."

Dr. King accepted the award for all the people who had crusaded with him. He said, "I accept this award in the spirit of a curator of some precious heirloom which he holds in trust for its true owners—all those to whom beauty is truth and truth beauty—and in whose eyes the beauty of genuine brotherhood and peace is more precious than diamonds or silver or gold."

Kings, queens, and international dignitaries stood to honor the peaceful crusader. After the ceremonies students honored him with a torchlight parade. A hero's reception greeted Dr. King in the other European countries he visited after the ceremonies.

A man of peace receives the Nobel Prize.

The Nobel Peace Prize consisted of a medallion, a diploma, and $54,600. Dr. King gave all the money away to help the freedom movement. He also gave away most of the money he earned from his books—to further education, religion, and freedom.

Many American cities honored Dr. King when he returned home. About 1,500 black and white citizens of Atlanta honored him with a banquet in a hotel ballroom.

Yoki, Marty, and Dexter were bright-eyed with excitement. They were almost too excited to stand up when they were introduced to the crowd. Dr. King was near tears as he thanked his friends. "I must confess that I have enjoyed being on this mountain top. I am tempted to stay here and retreat to a more quiet and serene life. But something within me reminds me that the valley calls me."

He returned to the "valley" to crusade for voting rights. Voting officials in the South often used hard tests, tricks, and threats to keep Negroes away from the polls. Dr. King inspired students to brave death and to lead Negroes in voter registration drives. He led peaceful "vote marches" to arouse the nation's concern.

His most famous vote march led from Selma, Alabama, to Montgomery, Alabama. Religious leaders and laymen of every race and faith joined the fifty-mile, four-day march. What a stirring sight it was! Hawaiians sent garlands of lei for the leaders to wear. Hand in hand with Coretta, Dr. King led 50,000 crusaders up to the state capitol.

Five months later President Johnson signed into law the 1965 Voting Rights Act. This act guaranteed equality and protection in voting.

The beginning of the march to Montgomery

"What now?" newsmen asked Dr. King.

"I must turn my attention to problems in the North," he answered. Northern states had a different kind of segregating wall. Negroes were crowded together in slums because their poverty and lack of good education made it hard for them to improve their living conditions. Dr. King began crusading for better homes, schools, jobs, and a chance for black and white children to know one another better.

Threats of death still came, from both the North and the South. White segregationists hated Dr. King for bringing about so many changes so fast. Many black men scorned him because they felt that his nonviolent methods were too meek. "I've conquered the fear of death," Dr. King often said. He taught his wife to free herself from fear too.

She did. "Someone has to pay the supreme price for progress," she said. She prepared the children. "Daddy may go to help people one day and never come back." The children understood.

Dr. King planned a massive crusade against poverty as his major project for 1968. He felt that all the nation's poor people should share in the good life

America offers. In March he went to Memphis, Tennessee, to help the garbage workers there in a march for better wages and working conditions. Some of the marchers became violent and began breaking store windows. The march had to be stopped.

Dr. King was saddened. It was the first time that he had not been able to control a march. "I must again prove that nonviolence *can* work," he declared.

"No!" friends urged him. "You may be killed."

Nevertheless Dr. King returned to Memphis a second time. On April 3 he spoke to a big crowd. ". . . I've been to the mountain top. . . . Mine eyes have seen the glory of the coming of the Lord."

12. The Last and Grandest March

It was another springtime in Atlanta. Freshly blossoming dogwoods displayed their vivid colors. Greenery unfolding everywhere gave promise of rebirth. The Easter season was nearing. The Dogwood City was about to be the scene of a drama unparalleled in American history.

Dr. King was still in Memphis. On April 4 he completed plans for a second Memphis march. A.D., also a preacher, was with his brother.

Late that afternoon Dr. King dressed for dinner. Looking fresh and handsome he stepped out onto his motel balcony.

He talked with Reverend Abernathy and other faithful SCLC aides. A gentle smile brightened his face.

Suddenly a shot rang out. Like his hero Gandhi, Dr. King was stopped in his crusade by assassination.

The crusader had taught his family well. Coretta first told Yoki, who was now grown-up enough to prefer being called by her real name, Yolanda. The twelve-year-old girl put her arms around her mother. "You're such a brave lady," she whispered. "I'm going to help you." Yolanda and her mother then told the other children. The children all understood. Their hero-father had died helping people, but his spirit would never die.

Four days later Yolanda, Marty, and Dexter walked beside their mother to lead the march Dr. King would have led. Holding hands, they led 20,000 silent marchers *peacefully* down the main street of Memphis.

The next day the children joined in the last and grandest march. Dr. King would have liked their courage. A newsman called Yolanda "a small madonna in white." Marty and Dexter stayed manfully erect. Even baby Bunny was quiet.

Martin Luther King led the march, even in death. His funeral march began with private services at Ebenezer. Ralph Abernathy, the minister who had followed his friend during the twelve years from Montgomery to Memphis, officiated. Even so, Dr. King was the main speaker. His recorded voice gave a sermon he had preached in Ebenezer only a few weeks before. He told how he wished to be remembered upon his death.

"Say that I was a drum major for peace."

The "last and grandest march" of all

A white-flowered cross and the American flag led the four-mile march to Morehouse for public services. All American flags flew at half-staff.

A faded green farm wagon, drawn by two mules, held Dr. King's casket. This simple wagon symbolized Dr. King's love for poor people. Behind the clip-clopping mules marched 200,000 men, women, and children.

It was like the March on Washington all over again. Presidential candidates marched beside penniless laborers. In the sad splendor of the day, marchers linked arms in song, friendship, and peace as Dr. King had taught them.

On the Morehouse campus familiar dogwoods shed their petals to make a carpet of honor. The Morehouse Glee Club sang the songs M.L. had sung as a student. Dr. Benjamin Mays, President of Morehouse, spoke in his familiar wisdom. ". . . it isn't how long one lives, but how well."

The march ended. The marchers sang a final promise to their fallen leader. "We shall overcome some day."

The dreamer was put to rest. Above his resting place are carved the words he used to end so many crusades. "FREE AT LAST, FREE AT LAST, THANK GOD ALMIGHTY I'M FREE AT LAST."

Dr. King lived to see part of his dream come true. For the walls of segregation had been so weakened that all races could learn to understand and love one another.

The gentle spiritual leader left a great lesson to the world. *You can protest without hating. You can struggle without violence. Love will outlast hate.*

Dreamers die, but dreams pass on. Dreams and ideas know no boundaries of race or time or place. Thoreau passed his ideas to Gandhi, who passed them along to an American dreamer named Martin Luther King. Dr. King wove the ideas into a dream for a better world— a world where all men might live in peace and love, without poverty.

Somewhere, sometime, perhaps someone else will make Dr. King's dream his own.